Staring Through My Eyes

poems by

Sylvia Cavanaugh

Finishing Line Press
Georgetown, Kentucky

Staring Through My Eyes

Copyright © 2016 by Sylvia Cavanaugh
ISBN 978-1-944899-79-0 First Edition
All rights reserved under International and Pan-American Copyright Conventions.
No part of this book may be reproduced in any manner whatsoever without written
permission from the publisher, except in the case of brief quotations embodied in critical
articles and reviews.

ACKNOWLEDGMENTS

"A Question of Locks," *Stoneboat Literary Journal*
"B-boys of Green Bay," and "Frank Juarez Gallery Tour," *Verse Wisconsin*
"Biker Bar," *Midwest Prairie Review*
"Breakdancers Take the Night Bus Home," and "Our Own Iliad Told,"
Verse-Virtual
"Cherry in Seattle," *Seems Literary Magazine*
"Detention," and "Woman...Man...Fish...Bicycle," *The Camel Saloon*
"Duplex," and "Stone Boy of Appalachia," *Making It Speak: Artists and Poets in Cahoots*
"Fort of Blankets," Songs of *Eretz Poetry Review*
"Hot Flash" *Red Cedar Review*
"Mermaid Tattoo Becomes Enmeshed in Her Relationship," *Peninsula Poets: Contest Edition*
"Mount Joy Homeless," *Peninsula Pulse*
"Rusted Houses," *An Ariel Anthology*
"Summer City Drift," *Burdock Magazine*

Publisher: Leah Maines

Editor: Christen Kincaid

Cover Art: Sylvia Cavanaugh

Author Photo: Grace L. Nicora

Cover Design: Elizabeth Maines

Printed in the USA on acid-free paper.
Order online: www.finishinglinepress.com
also available on amazon.com

Author inquiries and mail orders:
Finishing Line Press
P. O. Box 1626
Georgetown, Kentucky 40324
U. S. A.

Table of Contents

For Sarah Cavanaugh
My childhood of words

Stone Boy of Appalachia

An oblong stone
that was once a boy
who angered a woman
stares out
from the end of the yard
where auto frames
on cinder blocks
ease themselves to dust
their rusted coils
offer up
a nested last
resistance
lockjaw boy
stands mute

City cousins
run right past
to picnic as their mothers sweep
high on wooden swings
giggling into treetops
girlishly
and later on
to gawk
slack-jawed
at the strip-mined
vein
scraped right down
to the tendons
of the town

Rope Climb

Sun-filtered woods with their hard packed trails
meander their steep slope to the river
where an arched railroad bridge casts sun-wrought shade
from hand hewn stones of hazy men

trains sear civilization's untamed wound
tied to rails they sway rough clank through named towns
found the boy in me, the one I waited to love

I hurtle past accusation as Elvis on the radio
pleads plaintive truth of suspicious minds like this
rasp of burn hazel and how the sharp smell of weeds
permeates the breath of July's cicada whir
straight down the spine of afternoon

I prefer the uncaring face of this river to that
of the universe with its galaxies
in the water's particulate waste I taste the metal
of my blood as I steel myself against its forward press
my privacy cradled and cool caressed
the river's dark indifference saturates my need

today I fly across a slumped summer waterfall
to grab tight this spent rope, limpid-hung expectant
from the stone bridge, shoulderer of trains that
halt my breath and shudder my thoughts

I muscle my way up the thick twist of hemp
entranced by its endless double twine of self-embrace
hand over hand the rope now taut above me
rough scrapes my thighs to the holding clasp of feet
beneath the strain of bone and tendon
its frayed end swings the heavy spin of infinity

tonight I will join the women who lean
back into folding chairs and intertwine their
stories on the front stoops of houses fused
together with interlocking bricks

frosted lips will form words while legs cross one
over the other with the absentminded turn of ankle
to guide the dangle of pink polished toes
as they trace the slow arc of doubt

Rusted Houses

Uncle Jimmy hangs tin cans
collected from the dump
in branches of trees
for Appalachian birds
to raise their young
in suitable rusted enclosure

an unmarried miner
who spent his days
heaving to the score of metal notes
with his spindly arms
up against a face of coal

he picked up those cans
and strung them high

as a child from the city
I used to wonder why
he would broadcast
the trash like that

whirled into a galaxy
of chirping constellations

Fort of Blankets

Built over the sidewalk
in this neighborhood of no grass

where a massive chestnut tree
casts costly shade
over its choke collar of concrete
rust-brick houses press close

Beatrice invites me in
she's a little younger than me
I crouch down through the doorway
her bedroom blanket
auras rosy over my telling
of mountain stories
abandoned mills and mines
heavy revolvers
and dealings with spirits
the need to navigate the dark with care

she seems to like the part
about the spirits and the dark
asks for more
our limbs lazily touch

rough scrape of sidewalk
muffled thin as the comfort we spin
I know now that I want to kiss her
like a sister
but had no words for it then
blue eyes and brown
round as a settled world

Duplex

Duped by a rectangle of glass above the door
in the way its light came in
but we could not see out
like the eyeless yellow marigolds between our walks
all fringe with no insight
tough alchemy of the nearly defeated

sometimes a warmed patch of light drifted in
to land on dust mote winter days
we played with paper dolls

our fathers once re-shingled the dilapidated roof
outside our back doors were sets of stairs
they had agreed upon

edgy summers drummed time
the staccato whap whap of screen doors
our lives latched to the people next door
in the jumpy bang bang of summer

I used to dream of a house
I could run all the way around
timed myself over and over

we shared a chimney
devilish bats would echo their way
down its dusty tunnel
and then have to decide

sometimes we heard the neighbors' shrieks at night
and sometimes they heard ours.

Winter's Patchwork

Mother whispers
of her dreams
cut up
pinned down

to Clark Street
our brick house
boxed-in
by redundant
right angles
hedges
of twig-barren brown

we huddle
under her quilt
sewn from patches
of childhood dresses
like sun dogs
sun-spun
from crystal
prism paperweight

captured, stitched
and complicated
into a prison
of endless double
wedding band
design
traced soft
from meandering
ridges of fingers

Mount Joy Homeless

Solitary car dweller
rocked-out drop-out
once galloped alleyways
of honeysuckle summer

we were all storytellers back then
and he most of all
his exuberance would spin colors of taffy
to fill your mouth
cling to teeth the way we clutched our sides
in unbearable laughter
or like his butterflies pressed
under plates of glass
traced with fingers
he'd understand my impulse
to write this story
from my Midwestern prairie desk

of the unhinged Oldsmobile
just outside Mount Joy
left in the thicket of hemlock
beside November's chilly creek
as a boy he chased butterflies
through July's bright shimmer
and in his mind at night
tracked them to rocks
and fallen ledges
fairy hollows and mossy places

winter's first flakes
press down on the backs
of evergreen branches
as they reach wide their tips
in a graceful downward arc
alight with the weight of white

fifty three
alone in an abandoned car
tumbled from the flanks of joy
rusted blood slows its course
clutched in metamorphic heat
of snow

Summer City Drift

Fully petalled velvet
with overflowing scent
his brown suit
and the black bicycle
he rode to work
speak of it openly
the teenage girl across the street
who listened to Steppenwolf
in her basement
soft honeysuckle scent
accented the lazy cicada whir
a cascading metal ascent
of sound
red brick walls
red roses grew against
the Hungarian man
who lived around the corner
went to Woodstock
behind his faded white stable
the alley with its fool's gold
and fossilized horse dung
we picked up and examined
men in dark work pants kneeled
over roses in the dusk

Vietnamese Boy Meets Pennsylvania Girl on Jersey Beach, 1978

A languid land
terraced with grasses that sway
'round ancestor encrusted grounds
whose shrines gleam
in moonglow mango groves

seasons stream pathways
of birdsong dawn
down mother's tender tread

shoulders rise and fall
as his quavering language
glides and quivers
like a layering of notes
cascading
from a single metal string

helpless arms grace wide
his upturned palms
as he struggles for me to see
in English

downcast lashes shadow over
embarrassed laughter
and I begin to grasp
just how big
"beautiful" can be
in a distant slender home

on Jersey tidal backwater beach
brackish water laps toes
withholds its moonbeam trace

Biker Bar

I learned to ride a motorcycle
in a bid to save my marriage
my Honda Shadow trailed behind
exhaust fumes from his Harley

late afternoons
we undulated down
swerving country roads
through lilac scent that burst
its fenced-in borders
June-lit summer evenings
on the way to biker bars

where women amalgamate tendon-thin
on nicotine and high-heeled boots
and men without helmets
gather in gusts of raucous laughter

I never fit in
with my reflective safety vest
my husband always ditched me
when we rambled through the door

the vest was too big
stiff and awkward
made me visible in the dark

Our Own Iliad Told

Carried on motorcycles
to bars settled into hills
of glacial debris

a Vietnam vet overlooks
my reflective safety vest
to share a drink with me
his leather jacket
scraped thin at the seams

speaks of how he was Budweisered
every morning he had a mission
a case from the refrigerator
to help him climb into the cockpit

it was an equipment malfunction
that time the entire load dropped

he saw it from the thick air
like a buzzing in his head
or shimmer
his own company
on the ground

he turns over the story
seldom told
lays it down
between our glasses of beer
I pick it up
his pale gaze
I try to hold

B-boys of Green Bay

Asian b-boys in Green Bay
breakdance in Boys and Girls clubs
in Madison gyms they session, too
Menasha, Minneapolis, and Milwaukee

story re-writes itself in those who move
cultures fuse to dream anew
right foot lifts and steps aside
followed by the left
yet the center always holds
mid-western cyphers ground this dance
gravity partners with defiance
they fly in the placid face of it

South Bronx lynched in '70's style
freeway strangulation
fuels spontaneous combustion
Kafka jives to a Latin beat where
all that fly are colors
two turntables spin to just one song
layers of loose linoleum whirl helicopter legs
dizzy headspins on cardboard sheets
remnants of desire
windmills shrug off concrete floors

far to the west a mountain people
also lived on slash and burn 'til opium
smoked their crop to cash
alchemy of imperialism bespoke a
golden triangle
secret war and hidden trail
hunger's flight through clicking steps
landmines and helicopters hurling souls
scattering winds
extended clans gone nuclear

b-boy flies up off the floor
released from footwork, spins, and one-armed stands
statues himself to a landing freeze
integrity gestures to the ground
because all your pieces and all your steps
and the way in which you rock the beat
dance the very math of funk so that
two against three adds up to One

Breakdancers Take the Night Bus Home

An American advisor
for an Asian breakdancing crew
I inhabit the front of the bus
cruising through a winter storm

the driver rests wide and easy in his seat
casts out a few tales
casually over his shoulder

b-boys dwell in the realm
of gravity and weight
I wait through edgy encounter
with some Madison boys in McDonalds
the driver waits for a Florida vacation

bus ride home explodes
in a cacophony of white
firecracker photos snapped
on smartphones
uproarious defenses mounted
over flickers of images
arms over shoulders
sling them together

to sing the old songs
the words of their fathers
who once were young soldiers

they laugh at each other
for knowing the words

snow drives hard against the glass
night drives dark down the aisle
b-boys arc forward
and bring back
a forested mountain home

Frank Juarez Gallery Tour

Sweeping midwestern
landscape of apricotted sky
abstracted fields of line and color
freeways harvest
cornfield topography

art emotes land with gifted brush
third ward galleries brush against smoked
industrial valley
imagine charcoal

Frank Juarez our guide
from gallery to gallery
we cut through cream city alleys
patina-ed narrows where
windows squint through nailed-on boards
glance towards dumpster's
tilted lurch
his mama once worked in a factory here

alleys orient our compass
every time we step out
from their shadows
dazzling sunshine window glass
offsets brick along its detail craft
could have been Portland, Toronto, or
Atlanta

at lunch there are exotic
urban flavor drinks
martini-ed Motown
melodies wonderful
Frank Juarez shares his fries

Momma J

Momma J is a teacher
could be my teacher
she's my friend
she's my partner in crime
each day to the chime
of the bell
she's the yang to my yin

Momma J gets excited over African
curriculum
South Asian, too

Momma J with her life-size cutout of Gandhi
she shrieks and she screams
they've arrested Nehru's mother
and *word to your mother*

Momma J who howls history
from inside her story
as I hide in my room
her shoes of vermillion
like vermillion of a million
cities forbidden

click clack down the hall
when I hide in my room
Momma J who is presented
with bottles of Jack
at the bar on her birthday
from strangers admiring

Momma J with black eyes
from way down and deep
who knows stories of kids and venereal diseases
who collects your confessions
who forgives your transgressions

jive-boogies her way
with a cardboard cutout of Gandhi
Momma J
Momma J
Gandhiji

A Question of Locks

We always lived
so close to the pavement
summertime voices of walkers
strolling fragments down the street
Mother used to lock the door
and tuck us in at eight

these days my vision sprawls
over a landscape of scattered old farmhouses
white snow on flat fields
bounded at the edge by twig-barren scrub

floorboards creak unsteady
under an accumulation of drink
at night

I hover unhinged
behind the door
make sure it stays unlocked

Woman...Man...Fish...Bicycle

Perfectly round ova
nested within
were formed along with the rest of the body
in the shelter of a mother's space
from her own singular orb
round eggs round the chain of
life it clicks along
propels a forward tide

while men burrow down in furrows of
clone technologies make their
swimming cells redundant
whiplash tails
accidents of evolution
all come down to our bodies
our brains
and our inventions

like this red and gleaming two-wheeled frame
perfect fit between two legs
propulsion honed to hip and knee
press of foot and ankle flex
thumb and bell cry
we are coming
we are coming
self-satisfied we
cruise a moist planet
her many trails

Mermaid Tattoo Becomes Enmeshed in Her Relationship
Inspired by an art exhibit of tattoos from the 1940's

I was crafted carefully and with cunning
to link my ink to this relentless red flow
nailed down to the pulse
like a seashell ocean's echo my
two dimensions bend and arch
they ache to the rhythm of his three as
I'm plastered flat to a twining twitch
of muscle and deeper down
I sense the bone I cannot grasp it makes
my stomach turn and yet my
tiny nipples burn I yearn for him
trapped beneath the death of him
as his outer layer flakes away
and I'm the only witness

we hover over women with
their open legs like rowboat oars
the wretched separation
distantly they beg for us and
gnash their teeth
we heave and sweat
the salty sea and thrash
a flash of scale on
spangled tail
'til his eyes roll back
and stare through mine

Kaleidoscope: Glimpse of Vivian Maier

The film, Finding Vivian Maier, explored the life of Vivian Maier,
a gifted street photographer who worked in obscurity as a nanny.
Thousands of her undeveloped photos were discovered after her death.

I know about fear
the way it explodes, like the universe,
from a singularity of emptiness
rushes into the breathless void
and freefalls into the blank beam of
what comes next

I saw you on the silver screen
and your collected headlines of horror
grasped in a scissors' clutch
behind deadbolt doors
boxes of life's particles
like ticket stubs and buttons
a strewn galaxy of the unattached

and mostly your photographs
how they stun in an artflow of frozen humanity
I felt the camera against your heartspace
between frozen lungs
because fear fears its own breath
and what it may reveal

I imagine a kaleidoscope

undeveloped negatives filed away
like layers of emerald leaves
roles of film ambered in canister enclosure

one of your self-portraits
catches the shadow of your dark and manly coat
looming like a predator
and the image of your own small self
reflected in the silver cell of a garden sprinkler
the splinter chrome shine of you

nested in the veneer of man
in the place your womb would be

I imagine a kaleidoscope
when the jittery turn of wrist
engages broken glass
in its scrabbling slow-motion climb
to find purchase wrought from dizzy
flash and dazzle

lives plucked from a city street
gemstones of perception captured in pattern
formed for a breath
from beneath the cover of chaos

A Man

dresses like a woman
in Newark
walking to the poetry festival
no spectacle fantasy
of spike heels
tight-up Tinkerbell glitter

this man commands the pavement
like a Yoruba king cast in bronze
far-looking eyes
slant slightly in symmetrical
face bones
sealed lips speak the indigo cool
of discretion

this morning he donned a frock
I would wear in autumn
color of rustic leaf-spun rain
opaque tights
mahogany lace-up ankle boots

I wonder if this man in a dress
could be straight
could be a straight man
wearing a dress
because he likes the color
and the feel
the way I like to wear pants
sometimes
Could this be the start of fashion
without labels?

we smile at each other
a moment's validation flickers
between us

I want this moment to last
but his stride glides right past
the festival door
as I grab hold the handle
with one hand
lean back into sun and street

Cherry in Seattle

As if to keep your thoughts underground
fingers at the controls
free to feel for mineral spice

your past a part of the city scenery
another winter barren
under a shrouded sun
its light empty as film too soon unwound

the scraps of years hefted up
then shunted down

but springtime sap
heartless snake
refuses to stay put
seeps a bitter bile
creep of chill
beneath a fingernail

the hinged man of bone and tendon
who warmed your bed
dug in with greed of a thief
set you to bloom in open air
branch dark defiant hair
tattooed your blush in the heart of porcelain flounce

footfall of his stride
shook the earth to your core
to your outer edge
then gone

this annual ascent of sap scolds
like some sharp-tongued fisherman's wife
with her switch
ignores the pleas of gravity
of reason
of adrenaline rush
casts you to that ring where you feel it most
an amber stain
fiftieth circle counting in
next year fifty-first
still you blossom
in light
in shame
pull close the gossamer rain

Hot Flash

To forge weapons
with fire
is a sign that we are civilized
but the taste of knowledge
had its price
dealt in a currency
of fertility
in calendar clicks of counted days
a real blood bargain
paid periodically
paid in labor pains and
in pre-menstrual syndromes

but now I wield
my own damned fire
to cauterize the wound
the first sin settled up
my womb
now sweated caustic clean
Adam's bones are *mine*
and he is scorched
turning on these embers
he re-arranges and adjusts
looks at me
across his stiff
cold shoulder
and winks

Snowballs

I moved here as a young professional
on a January day
after a typical winter storm
drove down street after street
and in the yards
children built snowmen
from balls of glittering white
with everyone pitching in
to strain, push, and marvel, too
that individual flakes of snow
could become this drift
become this ball
become this man

years later, I walk with you
through the city at night
steamy houses breathe out
another summer's day

everything's quiet as shadows tilt
over slabs of pitted concrete
a big old snowball bush
spills out its strange exuberance

moonly orbs hover and float
with some internal electric glow
like an inspired conflagration
of a congregation of flowers
soldered together at the stem of things

the sight stops my heart
in its downward creep
we hold hands and start to talk
about how we love to be alone

James Joyce as Interventionist God

The earth leaned towards some solstice
that might have been joy
but the streets were black with drizzle
and barren enough to feel safe
I shoved my hands in my pockets
and followed a rumor to an old warehouse
where *Ulysses* was supposed to be read aloud
from start to finish in 24 hours

it was late in the evening when I joined
five other readers
drenched in an aura of artificial light
its stark beam honed on a tabletop
of Guinness bottles and day-old scones

obsolete words from a story without plot
self-indulgent, it seemed
traced to a time forgotten
when battlefields like Verdun
could script an aftermath of angst
            wrought from terrible lungs
            and pelted from the sky
onto what was once a new generation

a book to be hurled against the wall

one of the men reading that night
asked to be granted the last fifty lines
softly he spoke the words
as our world slipped into the indigo shadow
of a new day

and then he told us those last fifty lines
allowed him to forgive Joyce for all the rest

I thought, if there were an interventionist god
isn't this what we would pray for?
That he would grant us fifty lines good enough
we could forgive him all the rest?

I think of you, and the way we found each other
when you were already old and I was worn out
anachronistic, we thought
but just in time for those fifty lines

the summer we met I put the rose in my hair
like the Andalusian girls wore
and will somehow always wear
lying among the rhododendrons
(Does your heart go like mad in the reading?)

when we embraced I pulled you down and down
pressed to the lingering perfume of my breasts
Yes I said yes I will Yes

Sylvia Cavanaugh grew up in a red brick row house in Lancaster, Pennsylvania, with neighbors always close at hand. Her mother attended college and majored in English when Sylvia was young, and, being a poet, too, often recited poetry around the house. Irish coal mining relatives lived about an hour north, and the family frequently left the city to visit these immigrants in the mountains. There Sylvia encountered enormous trees that turned red and gold in fall, cavorting hoards of beagles, bee hives, introversion, tin cans strung up in trees, long abandoned Fords, a boy turned to stone, shotguns, and strip mining.

Sylvia attended undergraduate school in western Pennsylvania, then moved to the Midwest and earned her M.S. in Urban and Regional Planning from the University of Wisconsin. After working in health care planning and marketing for a few years, she went back to school to become a social studies teacher. She taught African American history and art in a Minneapolis high school for nine years, then returned to Wisconsin. She has taught African and Asian history and cultural studies for the past fifteen years in Sheboygan, and has been the advisor for the breakdancing and poetry clubs. She is fascinated with cultures, and the ways in which they move through populations and change over time.

Sylvia is the proud mother of three children, and although she read to them and shared her own tales as they were growing up, has always loved the ways in which they create their own stories.

www.ingramcontent.com/pod-product-compliance
Lightning Source LLC
LaVergne TN
LVHW041328080426
835513LV00008B/630

* 9 781944 899790 *